# A little light worrying

BOMBS FOUND ON PLANE!
TALKS FAIL
HOSTAGES KILLED
CRISIS: REACTOR LEAKS
JOBLESS UP!
IRISH TALKS: LITTLE HOPE
What's the problem?

Mel Calman

# A little light worrying

*The best of Mel Calman*

Selected and introduced by Claire Calman
with a preface by Michael Palin

Methuen

Published by Methuen 1997

1 3 5 7 9 10 8 6 4 2



First published in the United Kingdom in 1996 by Methuen London
Random House, 20 Vauxhall Bridge Road, London SW1V 2SA

Random House Australia (Pty) Limited
20 Alfred Street, Milsons Point, Sydney,
New South Wales 2061, Australia

Random House New Zealand Limited
18 Poland Road, Glenfield,
Auckland 10, New Zealand

Random House South Africa (Pty) Limited
Endulini, 5A Jubilee Road, Parktown 2193, South Africa

Random House UK Limited Reg No. 954009

**A CIP catalogue record for this book is available at the British Library**
ISBN 0-413-71440-3

Most of the drawings and texts included in this volume were originally
published in the following newspapers and magazines:

*The Times, Sunday Times, Daily Telegraph, Sunday Telegraph,*
*Town & Country* magazine

Many were subsequently published in book form in the following volumes:

*Bed-sit* (Jonathan Cape, 1963), *But it's my turn to leave you . . .* (Methuen, 1980),
*Calman & Women* (Jonathan Cape, 1967), *Calman Revisited* (Methuen, 1983),
*Calman's Savoy Sketchbook* (Aztec Design, 1994), *Couples* (The Workshop, 1972),
*Dr Calman's Dictionary of Psychoanalysis* (W. H. Allen, 1979),
*How about a little quarrel before bed?* (Methuen, 1981), *It's only you that's incompatible!* (Methuen, 1984), *Merrie England plc* (Mandarin Paperbacks, 1990),
*My God* (Souvenir Press, 1970; reissued Methuen, 1985), *The Big Novel* (Methuen, 1983),
*Through the Telephone Directory with Mel Calman* (Putnam & Co., 1962)

Typeset by Falcon Oast Graphic Art
Printed and bound in Great Britain
by Creative Print and Design (Wales), Ebbw Vale

*In memory of my father, Mel,*
*who enjoyed a little light worrying*

# Contents

# Preface

Mel Calman was seriously funny. His intense frown and grey, anxious features concealed a warm appreciative worldliness. His morose appearance was so at odds with his inquisitive wit that I used to wonder if he practised looking miserable because he thought it suited him better. The expression I associate with Mel is a smile. Mostly mine, but very often his as well.

I don't have to try very hard to remember him. His voice, his expression, his quick, alert, humorous glance come easily and clearly to mind. Wherever I am in the world I can, in the time it takes to say Mel Calman, be firmly ensconced in Manzi's Fish Restaurant in Leicester Square, full of the anticipation of good gossip which followed the ritual opening: 'Now what have you been up to, Palin?'

The closer I focus in on Mel the harder it is to accept the fact that I am in the past and not the present. He was a man with whom you could celebrate being alive. He was curious. He enjoyed company and conversation and keeping up to date. Mel had his favourite topics – newspapers, films, writing, Soho, women, new buildings, old buildings, wildly speculative arts ventures – but he was never a bore. He was that rare combination – a good listener and a good talker. I never spent a dull moment with him in my life. Even now, over a year and a half after his death I find myself noting things that I should like to share with Mel and having to remind myself with equal parts of irritation and regret that, however nice you are to Him, God does not make friends immortal.

I first met Mel in the middle of the Satirical Sixties when we were both recruited onto a pop show called *Now!*, produced by a provincial television company in Bristol. I was hired because I could do impersonations of Harold Wilson more cheaply than John Bird, and Mel was hired because, for a short period after the legendary Timothy Birdsall appeared on *That Was The Week That Was*, no new comedy programme worth its salt was without a resident cartoonist. *Now!*

became *Then!* quite quickly but Mel and I remained friends. We found each other funny even if no one else did.

One of Mel's qualities was that while he never appeared to push or prod a relationship along, he worked with a dogged, if diffident, persistence to steer his friends in directions he thought would be good for them. He had decided that I should write a children's book and that he should illustrate it. I ummed and ahhed and prevaricated but in the end he outwitted me in true Mel style. He suggested that my family and I join him and his daughter Claire for a weekend of wonderful food and good country air at one of his favourite bolt-holes – Ballymaloe House in Ireland. There, Mel timed his move perfectly. After lunch on the second day, I lay sinking into a sofa wondering aloud what could possibly make my life any better when he raised a mournful eyebrow my way and observed that only in such moments of true contentment were great children's books born. I've a recollection that he bought me a brandy to emphasise his point. (Mel, not a great man for the drink, generously acknowledged its beneficial effect on others.)

Whatever the details, his strategy worked. That afternoon in Ireland Mel turned me into a Children's Author. With characteristic generosity he then put me in touch with Caroline Holden, one of his protégées at The Workshop (which he had opened in 1970), to illustrate the book, as he felt his own style of illustration wasn't right. It was the start of an ongoing collaboration with Caroline. I suppose Mel could take the credit for starting two new careers *and* introducing me to one of the best hotels in Europe. The Workshop, incidentally, later became the Cartoon Gallery where Mel, aided by his indispensable right-hand woman, Pat Huntley, worked indefatigably to increase public appreciation of cartoons and cartoonists.

As an artist Mel's strength lay in knowing his own limitations. As far as I'm aware he left behind him no half-completed Sistine Chapels or undiscovered portraits of the Queen. Once he had settled on the Little Man – and his female counterpart, who is virtually identical save for the curly hair – he used them to say everything he wanted to say. The seemingly infinite variety of expression and body language that Mel could create from such minimally drawn characters is remarkable. It was his talent to make it look deceptively easy.

Mel's handwriting is as famous as his drawing. The handwritten captions share equal space in the frame. Mel enjoyed words and language and he wrote prose easily and unfussily. But for me the *bons mots* of his captions will remain his most enduring trademark. He found human behaviour endlessly curious, and was fascinated by those, like himself, who tried to make sense of it. His technique was to miniaturise. To reduce enormous amounts of verbiage into a bull's-eye of some half-dozen words. It could be his cartoon of the woman sitting up in bed and addressing her partner with the words, 'I'm not being negative. I'm saying "no" ', or the sad man on the couch asking 'What are the symptoms of happiness, doctor?'

In his writing, as in his drawing, Mel knew about precision. And he knew that it was the essence of the best humour.

Mel reminded me sometimes of Woody Allen. Both of them Jews working in largely Gentile worlds. Coming at their subjects from a different perspective. Able to make jokes others couldn't or didn't. Jokes about indecision and anxiety, inadequacy and incompatibility, sex and guilt. Jokes that showed a mind at work, jokes unashamedly informed by an intellect. Jokes that could touch all sorts of raw nerves.

But when all's said and done Mel was an original. A cartoonist with a voice that was fresh and urbane. His spare, economic observations of twentieth-century angst set him in a world apart from the prevailing *Punch* magazine ethos of Thelwell ponies and Russell Brockbank Brylcreemed smoothies and harked back to great names like Fougasse and Pont.

Mel wrote in his autobiography, *What Else Do You Do?*, that the Little Man was his alter ego. 'I don't know what I would do without him. I imagine he feels the same way about me.' The autobiographical element is what gives Mel's work a raw edge of honesty and an appeal that makes the Calman trademark stand out amongst those of his contemporaries. There may be some who were laugh-out-loud funnier than Mel and, though I seriously doubt it, some who were more prolific than Mel. But very few have made such a characteristic imprint on their times.

Michael Palin
October 1995

# Introduction

'I cannot remember ever deciding to become a cartoonist. I seem to have slid into it the way that some criminals say they slid onto the wrong side of the law . . .' my father wrote in his autobiography, *What Else Do You Do?* It is certainly not a profession likely to be suggested by most school careers officers, but it seemed tailor-made for my father's particular way of looking at the world.

Unlike the fathers of my schoolfriends who did incomprehensible, important-sounding things in offices, my father's work was visible, tangible, and simply around – completely part of who he was, not just the way he earned his living. Postcards always had a little drawing on them somewhere, perhaps a man talking to the aloof head of the Queen on the stamp or illustrating something he had seen. He scribbled small figures on the backs of envelopes (being loath to throw anything away, a persistent family trait . . .), doodles on restaurant napkins, and occasionally even – outrageous and daring in my childish eyes – on hotel linen tablecloths. Best of all, though, he drew on the walls. Having no flair, or love, for DIY, he regarded cracks, blemishes, and holes in any wall as permanent features, and they often prompted jokes and drawings that incorporated them. One figure, a man drawn around an old rusty nail hole where one eye would be, simply says 'OUCH!' When I couldn't sleep one night, for fear of spiders coming to get me in the dark, he drew a succession of spiders on the wall next to my bed. They were as absurd and unfrightening as only he could

make them, with ridiculous grins, and saying things like, 'I'm a silly spider. I love to scare little girls.'

This selection of my father's work, in keeping with his disdain for rigidity and over-organisation, will I hope be enjoyed more for its wit, quality, and variety than for its rigorously methodical approach. Many are examples of his unique brand of wry humour, his little man looking perplexed by life, but resigned to it; some, such as the drawings from *The Times*, show his gift for making a pointed comment, bringing a small-scale, human perspective to a large-scale issue; others have a slightly dark or surreal quality that was peculiarly his.

I have included some cartoons from his earliest books, partly to show how his work changed over the years, and also because they were already displaying his trademark, a combination of dry humour, gentle mockery, humanity, and gloom. *Bed-sit*, which first appeared in the diary pages of the *Sunday Telegraph*, brought to life the first incarnation of his famous little man.

Although Mel was probably best known for his single box cartoons, the *Couples* strips are still pointed, fresh, and amusing some thirty years after they first appeared in the *Sunday Times*. These double-decker strips, with an unspoken – and sometimes surreal or symbolic – subtext drawn beneath the 'real' action, add another dimension to the work.

The cartoons from *The Times* were probably the hardest to choose. There is an inherent problem with topical and political cartoons: many that are sharp and funny at the time do not necessarily survive well. Mel's best ones are still funny years later, and either self-contained or so on the button that the joke itself also calls to mind the event that prompted it. Included here, inevitably, is only a tiny selection that can hardly hope to do justice to almost fifteen years' drawing.

Some people may think I show a lamentable want of taste in including my father's series of articles, 'Affairs of the Heart', about his heart problem, because he did finally die of heart disease. I also read out one of these pieces at the memorial we held to celebrate his life, feeling it matched his own enjoyment of black humour very well. Now, it's true, the pieces have an added poignancy, which perhaps makes them even more important to include.

He was interested in a huge variety of subjects: two projects in progress when he died were *Short Cuts* (1995), created with his friend Ben Duncan, a book for English language students, and *Calman's Savoy Sketchbook* (1994), a behind-the-scenes look at the Savoy Hotel. A few of his cartoons have also been produced as postage stamps by the Royal Mail.

In his entry in *Who's Who*, my father listed his interests as 'brooding and worrying'. While selecting cartoons for the book, I came across an early drawing from *Bed-sit*. Seeing it (and thinking of the publisher badgering me for a title), I knew it was the right title for this book, capturing Mel's lugubrious expression and his bemused view of life, love, and politics.

*I think I'll do a little light worrying . . .*

Claire Calman

# The early years

These drawings have been selected from four of Calman's earliest books, dating from 1962 to 1972.

*Through the Telephone Directory with Mel Calman* (1962): Mel hated waste, so when he moved into a flat containing an old, semi-ravaged telephone directory, he didn't throw it away. 'One morning, I cut up some of the entries and collaged them into a handful of cartoons . . .' His first book was begun. The style for London phone numbers – losing their prefix of letters to denote area – changed along with his drawing style.

*Bed-sit* (1963): First created for the diary page of the *Sunday Telegraph* in 1962, this panel cartoon used the outline of its own box to suggest the confines of a bed-sit. It was inhabited by a tenant who was the beginning of the distinctive little man: 'His views and opinions coincided in many ways with mine, but where I would be angry, he preferred to shrug his shoulders and mutter some wry aphorism.'

*Calman & Women* (1967): The start of Mel's lifelong preoccupation with the ups and downs (mostly downs) of the relationship between the sexes. This also saw some early examples of cartoons that were purely graphic, such as the love-is-blind man with heart glasses (coloured red in the original).

*Couples* (1972): This double-decker strip first appeared in the *Sunday Times* and was 'an attempt to explore the gap between what people say and what they think'. The bottom half sometimes shows the dynamics of the couple's relationship symbolically, with the man and woman going up and down on a see-saw, for example, as each scores verbal points off the other.

# *Through the Telephone Directory with Mel Calman*

*Normally, I'm afraid your qualifications would not be adequate, but when one is short of staff and the Smith season is on . . .*

*Say who you are –*
*do not just say 'Hello'*

"Salutation,"
" Ship," Wormwood st EC2....
" Swan," Ship Tavern pass EC3.....
" Swiss Cottage," 98 Finchley rd NW.
(General Public) ......................
" The Bath House," 96 Dean st W1.....
" The Champion," Wells st Oxford st W1
" The George," 55 Great Portland st W1
Do. ....................................
" The Magog," 8 Russia rw EC2.........
Do. ....................................
" The Salisbury," 90 St Martins la WC2.
Do. ....................................
" The White Horse," 1 Lee High rd SE1.
" The Yorker," 189 Piccadilly W1.....
" Yorkshire Grey," Theobalds rd WC1...
" Yorkshire Grey," 2 Theobalds rd WC1

# *Bed-sit*

*It may be small
but the proportions
are pleasing . . .*

*The landlady doesn't like the word 'restrictions'. She calls them 'aids to communal living'*

*The girl next door never seems to run out of anything*

*We depressives are entitled to a little bit of manic now and then . . .*

I think
I'll ring
the office
and say
I'm dead . . .

# *Calman & Women*

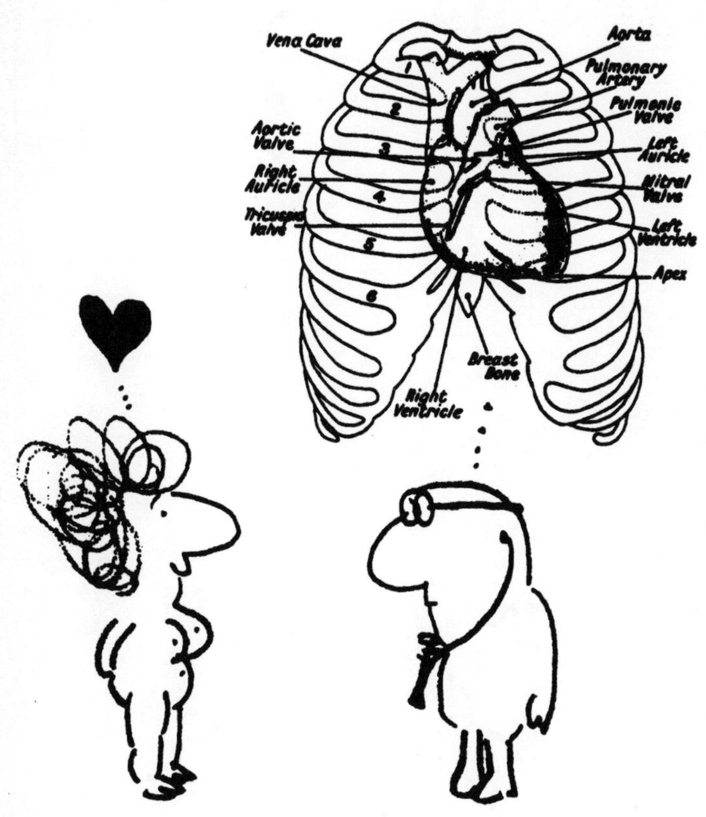
Vena Cava
Aorta
Pulmonary Artery
Pulmonic Valve
Aortic Valve
Left Auricle
Right Auricle
Mitral Valve
Tricuspid Valve
Left Ventricle
Apex
Breast Bone
Right Ventricle
1
2
3
4
5
6

Hello darling!
it's me

Oh- which me is that?

Femme
Fatale
OPEN
DAILY →

I think women need a sense of purpose in life

it's going to fall-
and it's your
fault

The last time I went into one of those it took me five years to get out...

The butcher said I was beautiful today
SUNDAY TIMES
He says that to all his women customers
He also asked how my father was
Your father??
He meant you...

Aren't you ready yet?
No!
A nice clean quarrel..
You're never ready on time!
I'm trying to make myself look nice–
No wonder it takes so long..
FOUL!
Below the belt!
FOUL!

She's late-
She's with a lover!
...or had an accident!
Sorry-hope
you didn't
worry..
Not at all..

Daydreaming again?
Fantasies are all very well, but I bet she can't cook as well as I can..
That's O.K.– you can do the catering...

What are you thinking?
Nothing..
If I catch you having sexual fantasies, I'll –
You'll what?
I'll join you...
?

Yes.. yes.. mm..
mm.. yes, of course...
Who was that?
-Just a wrong number..
Who can she be talking to? A friend?
or a lover?
Is that the truth? Should I pretend to believe her..
Someone, somewhere is doubting me...

When we first met you used to love listening to me
it's all different now, isn't it?
Yes, it is–
In those days you used to talk about me..
Rosie told me that Maurice has left Mary to join a monastery..
Hear no, see no & speak no gossip..

That's it!
I'm going..
As soon as I start packing she'll ask me to stay..
Where's my blue shirt?
I don't know!
I'm packing! say 'STAY'..
NO!
I can't go without my blue shirt - so I'll have to stay
How to stay without Losing Face..'

# Troubles with my Aunt

These pieces, which first appeared in the *Sunday Telegraph* magazine in 1974, now read almost like short stories. But they were indeed based on Mel's aunt, his mother's sister, Rebecca Marcus, who lived with him for some years. I certainly remember her bedtime trays with their paper-hatted cups of water from when I was a child. Now, her 'bequest' to Mel that he should not visit Russia, Finland, etc. seems strangely touching as well as funny. It was a serious matter to her, however, for she had escaped as a child from Russia with her mother and sister and they had been shot at as they crossed the border.

## *Paper bags*

My aged Aunt saves paper bags. I don't mean that she puts one or two away in a drawer for a rainy day. We all do that. I mean she keeps every single paper bag that comes into the house. She unwraps the bread and carefully puts the bag in a drawer. She places the bags from the groceries in the same drawer. She has a system: the brown bags in one drawer and the white bags in another drawer.

She usually puts the small bags inside the largest bags, to save space. Bags lie on top of bags. Bags nestle inside bags. Bags beget bags. Whole communes of bags live inside those kitchen drawers.

I ask my Aunt, when I feel slightly frayed by all this bag cupidity, why she keeps all these bags. 'I need them,' she says, and the subject is closed. To be fair to her, she does use some of the bags. Let me explain.

Every night my Aunt prepares her bedtime tray. This tray is a ritual, an appeasement to the gods of sleep. The pink tray is placed beside the kitchen sink. My Aunt carefully takes three cups and half-fills them with cold water. Always three cups, always the same three cups. And always half-full. Never three-quarters or five-eighths.

Exactly half. They are half-full because my Aunt has worked out over the years that a half-cup is exactly the right amount she needs to ease her heartburn. She gets attacks of heartburn in the middle of the night and she drinks fruit salts for this. A full cup of fruit salts is too much of a good thing. And she needs this cure three times a night. Hence, the three cups.

Ah, you may ask, why not a jug and three empty cups? Or even, a jug and one cup, which then gets half-filled three times? Because, as my Aunt patiently explained to me once, this method is foolproof and ready for use. It's an instant heartburn kit. No messing about in the half-light, trying to half-fill cups.

I once bought a jug and tried to persuade her to change her system, and she gave me a long, level stare that said: Never meddle with the laws of nature . . .

What about the paper bags, you cry. How do the paper bags cure the heartburn? Has the man lost all sense of narrative shape and decency? No. The paper bags are carefully torn open, flattened and used to cover the cups (or half-cups) of water. Each half-cup has its own little nightcap of paper, held down by a rubber band. And of course, they are needed to keep the dust out. My Aunt doesn't want dust getting into her water. Who would?

The problem is that even with using three bags a night, my Aunt is stockpiling bags rather rapidly. The drawers are full. I'm thinking of buying her a suitcase to keep the rest of her collection. But my Aunt doesn't approve of suitcases. Dust gets into them, she says. She admits that dust even gets into drawers. Which is why she gets the bags out every other day and dusts them. Gives them a careful dust, and then returns them to their correct drawer.

I believe my Aunt keeps these bags the way other old people have pets. Something to care for and look after. Not much company, perhaps. But at least house-trained. And, thankfully, very quiet.

## *Depressions*

My Aunt and I suffered a great deal from depression, mostly hers. When she felt depressed she would come into my room – where I was usually looking at a blank sheet of paper, hoping a joke would appear on it – and sigh.

'What's the matter, Auntie?'

'I feel terrible.'

'Take a tranquillizer.'

'Do you think I should? Who knows what's in them?'

'Neither of us knows. Just take one and you'll feel better.'

'It may make me feel worse.'

'You always take them, and you always feel better.'

'I don't think they're the same ones as the last ones the doctor gave me.'

'Of course they are . . .'

'How do you know?'

'They look the same. Green and black. With your name on the bottle.'

'They don't taste the same. Perhaps the chemist has given me the wrong pills.'

'Take one, please . . .'

Sigh. 'You think I should?'

'Yes, I do.'

'Doctors. What do they know?'

As my Aunt got older she suffered more and more from hypochondria (which must be hereditary, because I get it too – especially in the middle of the night) and needed more and more to consult doctors, in spite of her basic lack of faith in them.

Days would start and end with my Aunt asking me to call a doctor because she felt 'terrible'. If the doctor came, she would repeat all her ailments and troubles. He would listen patiently, leave a prescription, and I would go to the chemist with it.

Whatever was prescribed, my Aunt would distrust it. Look at it, sniff it, and worry whether it would make her worse. She would snort. 'What do doctors know? My mother, bless her, knew more in her little finger than these young kids know in their whole heads . . .'

'Why get me to call the doctor then?'

'What do you want me to do? Suffer in silence?'

Whatever else my Aunt did, she certainly never suffered in silence. She suffered her anxieties and depressions out loud. She crossed each day gingerly, as if it were a tightrope which might snap under her at any moment, and plunge her to her death.

The mornings began with sighs and remarks about how badly she slept the night before.

'I went to bed late again last night,' she would say.

'Really, why?'

'I started thinking about your mother and how she never looked after herself properly. If she had listened to me, she would still be alive. Always rushing about, doing things, enjoying herself. She should have rested her heart more.'

'Well, she did live to be seventy-eight. That's not too bad.'

'She could have lived another twenty years, if she had listened to me.'

'Her doctor said . . .'

'What do doctors know? Nothing.'

Then came breakfast of cups of tea and cream crackers. (Always Jacobs'. I once tried to palm her off with another brand and she sulked all day.) Then more sighs and heartburn. Treatment for heartburn with fruit salts, and more cups of tea.

More heartburn would follow the cups of tea. More anxiety would follow the heartburn.

'Do you think I've got an ulcer?' she would ask me, clutching her stomach.

'Of course not. But I shouldn't drink so much tea. It can't be good for your stomach.'

'Perhaps I should see a Specialist?'

'What kind of Specialist?'

'Someone who specializes in everything.'

'Just take a tranquillizer.'

'Do you think I should?'

'Yes, for God's sake, yes.'

'It might make me feel worse . . .'

How I wished there was a pill she could have taken to make her calm enough to take her tranquillizers . . .

## *At home with my Aunt*

My Aunt lived with me for several years in a small flat in London until she needed the kind of nursing that only nursing homes provide. And even they cannot always provide it. The aged (especially my aged Aunt) require their nurses to have a combination of endless patience, good humour and energy. Since I have nearly none of these qualities, I tried to find a suitable place where my Aunt could feel at home. But a Home was the last place where she could feel that emotion.

She tried several Homes. Or they tried her. They found each other trying, is the accurate way to describe the process. The first one was rather grand and in Surrey. It seemed to be a charming place. She went there on two weeks' probation, and was released early. I think she got time off for bad behaviour. The Matron gave me the impression that Her ways were not Their ways and never the twain would meet.

I collected my Aunt, like an unwanted present, and we returned to my flat. A friend mentioned a private place in Middlesex, just outside London. This turned out to be a badly organized affair, with inefficient nursing and no heating during winter. They also managed to put my

Aunt near a lady who was under the impression that the home was in Ireland. Whenever I went to visit my Aunt (while I feverishly looked for some alternative accommodation), she would beg me to take her away from Ireland.

'Why have you sent me to Ireland?'

'It's not Ireland,' I said. 'It's Middlesex.'

'The woman said it was Ireland.'

'She's mistaken.'

'I don't want to be in Ireland. The children will never come and see me.'

'Look – if she said this was Moscow, that wouldn't make it Moscow, would it?'

It made no difference. For the next few years, my Aunt would still reproach me for that episode.

'I'll never forget that dreadful time you sent me to that place in Ireland. Why did you do that? How could you put me so far away from London?'

'It was Middlesex.'

'Ireland. Terrible, terrible. How could you do that? If your mother was still alive, you wouldn't have done that to me . . .'

Then we tried a council home, which was even worse. It was run on Dickensian principles with just a hint of the penal settlement added. On arrival all her personal belongings were taken away from her, including her radio, so that they could be marked with her name. It may have made administrative sense, but it was a rotten way to welcome guests. No one was allowed to lie on their beds during the daytime. Unless they were dying. 'I don't like this place,' said my Aunt, 'it's full of old people.'

Finally and thankfully, another friend recommended a nursing home in North London, and my Aunt settled there. She shared a room with two other old ladies, and made a small barricade of her belongings and photographs round her bed as a defence against their intrusions.

She quickly tested the home and its staff by insisting that her laundry went to the same one she had been using all her life. This firm did not visit that district, so the Matron devised an ingenious stratagem of using my Aunt's old laundry boxes each week; taking the laundry to the local launderette, and then carefully returning it to her in the familiar boxes. She never suspected the truth.

She stayed there for several years, until one day the Matron phoned me to say that my Aunt was fading. She lay on her bed, very thin and barely present. She hardly ate anything, except some ice cream and warm milk. 'One day I'll go out like that light,' she said, pointing to the bulb above her head.

She took three months to fade into death. A certain stubbornness kept her alive, even though she was now ninety-three years old. I expect she is still stubborn in heaven, arguing with the staff and telling them not to send her wings to the wrong laundry.

*Baths*

Once a week my Aunt would announce, 'I am going to have My Bath today.'

Now most people find it fairly simple to have a bath. You probably remember how it goes. You enter the bathroom, you put the plug in, turn on the hot water, get into the bath, wash, sing, get out, dry yourself and exit. My Aunt's approach was more Epic, like one of those long Eisenstein movies where people seem to be forever climbing up the same flight of stairs.

My Aunt would first slowly collect her clean linen, so as to have it all ready for changing into after Her Bath. This involved Sorting Out her linen, which took up most of the morning. Sometimes she would find an old letter buried amongst her linen, become interested in the memories it aroused and have to postpone The Bath until the next day. But if all went well, she would have a bite of lunch and start Phase Two around two o'clock.

Phase Two was Washing Out the Bath. She had a great fetish about cleanliness, which I imagine was sexual in origin, since she was a maiden Aunt. I am sure Freud would have enjoyed analysing her motives – all I know is that it was very heavy on the Vim. She would wash the bath very thoroughly, rinse it with running cold water, rewash it and then carefully feel the whole surface with her fingers. If there was the slightest blemish, she would clean the whole bath out again. This took about an hour. Then she would fill the bath.

By this time she was feeling a bit hungry and exhausted. So she would put on the kettle for a cup of tea. Several cups of tea and several cream crackers (her favourite food) later, she would go back to the bathroom. And find the water stone cold.

So she would have to empty the bath and re-fill it. While it was filling, she would go to collect her Clean Linen. She carried all her underclothes carefully wrapped up in an old piece of torn sheet, tied and sealed with several safety-pins. I don't know why they had to be wrapped up like this since the distance between her bedroom and the bathroom was all of five yards. I think it was in case dust (one of my Aunt's great enemies) got at the clean linen.

At last she was actually ready for Phase Three – The Bath itself. Before she entered the water, she would call out to me that she was going in (in case I had not noticed she was Having a Bath) and that she was leaving the door unlocked in case she felt faint and needed sudden rescuing from drowning.

I would then settle down to work, and she would call out again. 'Can you shut the window? I can't lift it and I can't have a draught blowing down on me in the bath.' She always liked the window open whilst running the bath, to allow the gas fumes from the Ascot to escape, and she would always then need the window shut before she could enjoy the bath.

About an hour later she would slowly emerge from the steamy bathroom, carefully swathed in clean underwear and towels. (For some other deep Freudian reason unknown to me, my Aunt never owned, and could never be persuaded to buy, any kind of dressing-gown. I think she thought they were only worn by Loose Women.)

'Be a good boy,' she would say, 'and make me a nice cup of tea. I feel faint. The bath was far too hot.' Or sometimes it was, 'I feel faint and cold. I think I caught a chill in there.'

I would make us a pot of tea and she would drink it greedily, and sigh, as if just rescued from a sinking ship. She looked rather like a survivor, all wrapped in towels and exuding dampness. 'Thank God that's done,' she said. 'It's a terrible business, having a bath.'

## *Letter from my Aunt*

During her lifetime my Aunt wrote me several letters, many of them just short notes when she was living in an old ladies' home in North London. They usually were complaints about her health, or simply instructions.

I have one which is fairly typical. It is written on the back of an old envelope. The handwriting is slightly shaky, but very neat, in old-fashioned copperplate. This is the letter, in its entirety.

> Dear Melville (that's what she always called me),
> When you come, please bring all the necessary things:
> My Winter coat
> my winter dressing-gown
> mamma's summer dress
> everything from the Ilford laundry
> on the bed there is also an autumn coat
> which I may need.
> Monte said he may come to see me, so he
> should have the key
> so that he can take certain things which
> he may need, and to which he is entitled to,
> such as a
> Russian dictionary
> etc. Auntie

Here is another letter, this time written on proper blue notepaper.

Dear Melville,

I was going to phone to you and explain conditions, as writing is difficult for me. What I want to explain is that to the Ilford I send only things I ware to my body (by the way my spelling is bad). I send 1) my face towel, 2) my vest, my nightdresses and my bøath towels. This I do every week. Dresses are washed here, but dresses I only change once a month. So I do not make expenses. Recently I have another unpleasant feeling. I have an inpleasant feeling in my stomach. When you will come I hope I shall tell you details.

The favour I want you to do is to bring all my things and the dresses for which I paid 2 pounds for having them altered. They are nice and soft and pleasant. Why should they hang there. The things I have here are coarse and unpleasant. I feel very depressed.

Thanking you in anticipation,

Auntie

Towards the end of her life she sent me her will. It was written on one sheet of blue notepaper.

It was headed *My Will.*

To my nephew I bequeath my books and Russian Dictionary. To my nephew Melville I bequeath that he must never visit Russia, Finland or East Germany.

signed: R. Marcus.

It was dated and witnessed by one of the nurses.

# On the couch

I hope I'm not boring you.

Mel was always interested in health, and especially in psychiatry, depression, and various sub-species of gloom. They frequently cropped up in his work. He illustrated books on the subject and produced one of his own, *Dr Calman's Dictionary of Psychoanalysis* (1979), from which the psychiatr jokes in this section are taken.

Doctor - I keep feeling people are ignoring me!

Mm.. quite so..

Playboy

And stop reading articles on Health...
DOCTOR

I'm rather busy today - cant you be ill tomorrow?
DOCTOR

*Dr Calman's*
*Dictionary of Psychoanalysis*

## Analyst

My analyst doesn't understand me...

# Communication

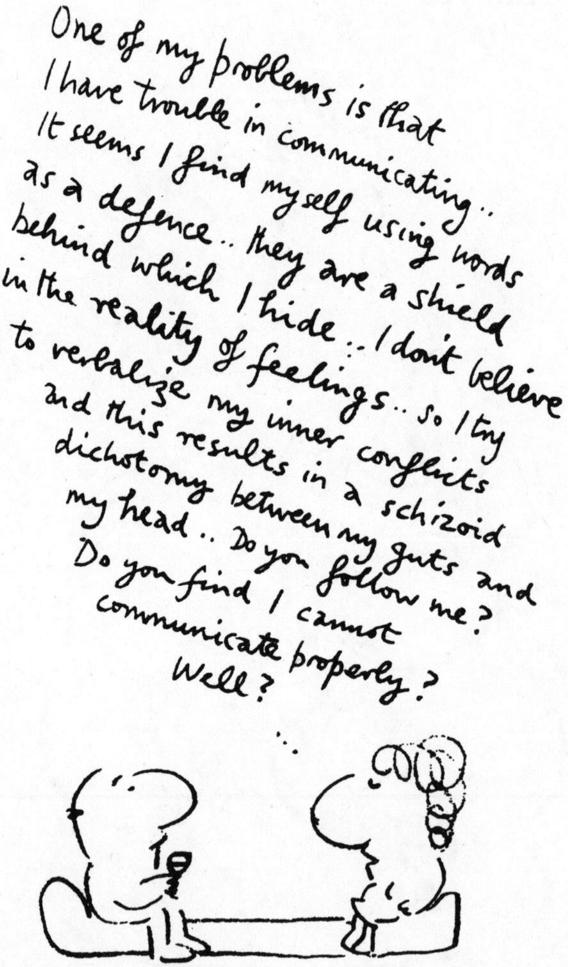

One of my problems is that
I have trouble in communicating..
It seems I find myself using words
as a defence.. they are a shield
behind which I hide.. I don't believe
in the reality of feelings.. so I try
to verbalize my inner conflicts
and this results in a schizoid
dichotomy between my guts and
my head.. Do you follow me?
Do you find I cannot
communicate properly?
Well?

...

# Dreams

## Free Association

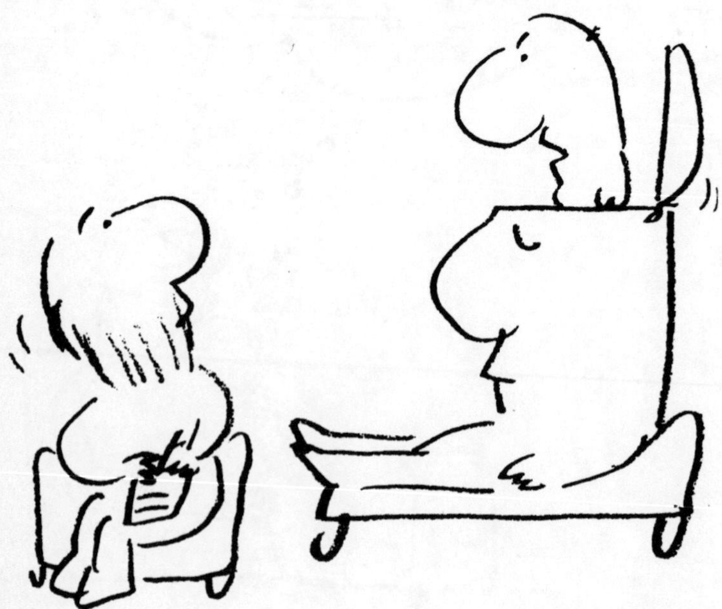

# Infantile Regression

Don't worry -
I've had worse cases..

# Love

When you say LOVE
do you mean EROS or
a need for instinctual
satisfaction or object love
or oedipal love
or genital love
or simple old-fashioned
schmaltz?

# Negative

I'm not being negative
I'm saying 'No'

# Obsession

The nature of obsession is very interesting. Obsessional thoughts express a need to control your impulses (see sex).. and I do wish you would wash your hands before you come next time as the germs tend to spread all over my couch and the next patient might contract your social diseases... now what was I saying?

Phallic Symbol

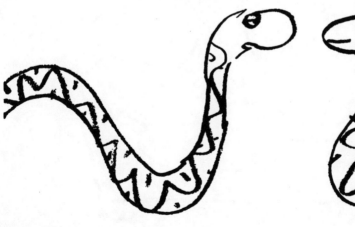

I dreamed of
a tall, dark man
last night

It's probably
phallic.

# Psyche

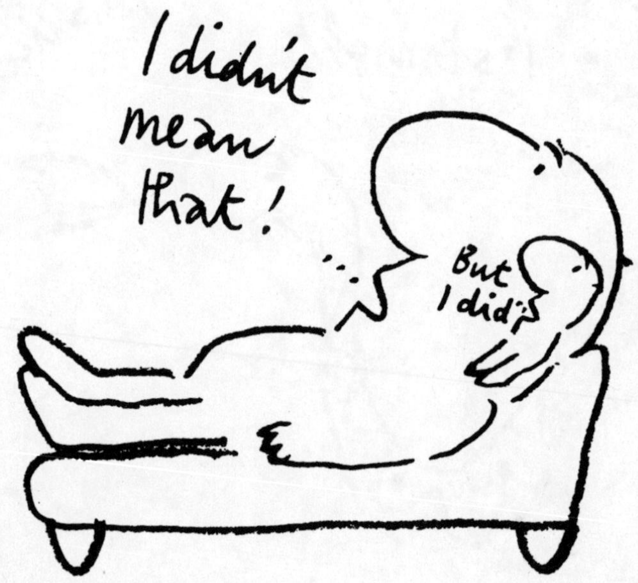

# Religion

# Sadness (*see* Gloom, Depression)

# Men and women

But it's my turn
to leave you

Most of these cartoons were originally drawn for the Field Newspaper Syndicate in America, and appeared across the United States six days a week for five years under the title 'Men & Women'. Later, some of them were collected in three books: *But it's my turn to leave you . . .* (1980), *How about a little quarrel before bed?* (1981), and *It's only you that's incompatible!* (1984).

'I was excited and terrified,' wrote Mel, when he first starte drawing for the syndicate. 'It felt like being something very close to a professional – and the thought kept me awake at nights. I preferred to think of myself as a gifted amateur – a man who somehow managed to get his work printed, in spite of his failings.'

Many of these are among my favourite of my father's cartoons; his pithy observations on the great divide of misunderstanding between the sexes still seem fresh, funny, and relevant. One of his best-loved jokes is the one with the woman bearing a placard proclaiming 'Free women now'; a rather smaller man is asking hopefully, 'Can I have one?'

How about a little
quarrel before
BED?

I demand
a second opinion..

I know she
LOVES me- by the
way she hangs
up..

Being a failure isn't as easy as it looks...

Why should I phone him?
I ALWAYS phone him..
And he's probably not in..
ALWAYS OUT doing things-
enjoying himself..
He never phones me.
I wish he would just
ONCE phone me..
I'll give him five more
minutes and then
I'm going out!

She hasn't phoned!
What's wrong?

I'm only his wife - his movements are beyond my jurisdiction..

WHY haven't we quarreled recently-
is something WRONG?

Would you pass
the conversation,
please?

I think I could
make you unhappy-
if you'd like
that..

I wish she were
here to annoy
me . .

Stop saying
nothing in such
an aggressive
voice . . .

THANK YOU
for
NOT SNORING.

We'd be happier
if you'd married
a millionaire..

I keep telling
him he LOVES me-
but he won't
listen..

I've just remembered- we're divorced!

Is there life after marriage?
LIFE after DEATH

It's only you that's incompatible...

I think she wants more than an apology...

And don't talk to me
until you're ready
to listen!

I'm too old for etchings –
but come up
anyway –

This is silly -
we can't BOTH
leave..

I related to
you yesterday -
today I'm
resting...

so I said –
Little does she know that I've been deaf for the past 5 ye...

A nice, clean fight with no undermining each other's egos..

Even a quarrel would be better than this..

One of us has to make the decisions and I've decided its me..

My accountant wants us to stay together..

Do you know of someone I could leave you for?

Let's compromise-
and say I'm right.

I'm RESTING before
I have to go out and
PRETEND to be
GROWN UP...

ORGASMS
HIS
HERS

I'm going to live
an independent life -
as soon as you've
packed my bags..

What do you
REALLY
want?

I want you to know
without my
telling you..

You don't understand women
You never let me meet any

I seem to bring out the lawyer in a woman...

My WIFE hasn't spoken to me for three days...

Perhaps she's trying to tell you something...

It's your turn
to be mature...

He's been completely
unspoilt by
failure

I've decided NOT
to renew my
subscription
with you this
year...

This is NOT
a SYMBOLIC GESTURE-
I'm leaving!

You're so OLD
that girl wasn't even
offended when
you leered at her...

The trouble with marriage is that it has deprived me of adult conversation..
ZZZ

I'm looking forward to getting home and complaining about the other guests..

I hated the play but I loved the way you kicked that man to get to the bar...

Your trouble is that your wife understands you...

And now she's threatening to stay...

We deserve to be MORE equal than MEN...

I remember you-
the first man to make
me UNHAPPY...

I'd like
a nice hobby..
You're got
your
arguing..

Will you be able to support a second wife in the style to which your first wife is accustomed?

I got custody of the bank loan..

Whatever happened to all your old feminine wiles?

One man's meat is another WOMAN'S SUNDAY gone . . .

Remember, dear-
it takes two
to make a quarrel..
Only if
You're an
amateur..

I said-
NOTHING'S
WRONG!
Oh dear-
it's worse
than I thought..

How can
I have the last word -
if she doesn't
phone me?

You're greedy, hostile,
depressed, childish,
selfish, angry,
moody, mean,
jealous,
difficult
and
... IMPOSSIBLE!

She CARES!

I hope my
EATING isn't
spoiling your cigar

Well?
If I say I liked it - will you promise not to give it to me again?

Jogging is like marriage - tiring but good for you...

Do you have something for the HUMAN CONDITION?

If They MESS it up -
we're NOWHERE
else to go...
SAVE
THE
PLANET.

If you really loved me - you'd go and hold the aerial...

She's upstairs - changing her mind...

I'm waiting
for her to call-
then I won't
answer it ...

He's out looking for
his lost youth - so
he'll be a long
time...

So - how was it for you?

How was what?

FREE WOMEN NOW!
Can I have one?

# Signs of *The Times*

When Mel first started drawing for *The Times*, in 1979, he was also producing a weekly topical cartoon for the *Sunday Times*, which he had been doing since October 1969. He drew a cartoon for *The Times* four days a week up until he died. His last cartoon, a comment on further NHS controversy, was a man lying in a hospital bed, saying: 'I hear this place is even sicker than I am.' It appeared in the first edition of the paper only; the second edition carried on the front page a photograph of him with the news of his death.

11 March 1987

1 April 1987

16 July 1987

19 August 1987

26 August 1987

23 September 1987

20 October 1987

31 December 1987

20 January 1988

10 February 1988

24 February 1988

5 April 1988

30 June 1988

12 January 1989

19 January 1989

23 February 1989

30 March 1989

25 April 1989

7 June 1989

18 July 1989

31 August 1989

13 September 1989

10 November 1989

14 November 1989

(OFFERED but PROBABLY UNUSABLE...)

28 February 1990. Sometimes the best cartoons are too close to the bone: the cartoon on the previous page was not used – Mel's comment shows he knew it might not make it. This one, though less pointed and funny, was used.

26 April 1990

9 May 1990

24 May 1990

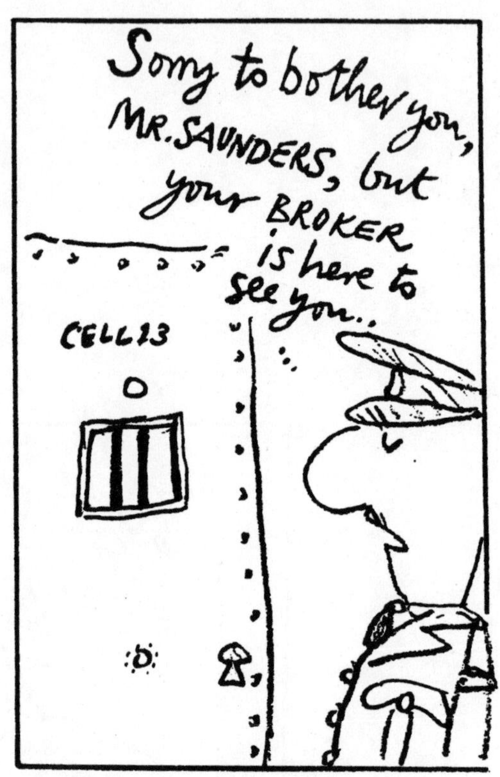


31 August 1990: Ernest Saunders, found guilty of 'price-rigging' Guinness shares

18 October 1990

26 October 1990

19 December 1990

15 January 1991

12 February 1991

13 February 1991

20 March 1991

Probably wants to
spend more time
with
grown-ups

SPEAKER
TO
RESIGN!

8 March 1991

3 May 1991

19 April 1991

12 June 1991

19 June 1991

24 July 1991

25 July 1991

8 October 1991

29 November 1991

12 December 1991

27 February 1992

The Budget,
March 1992

31 March 1992

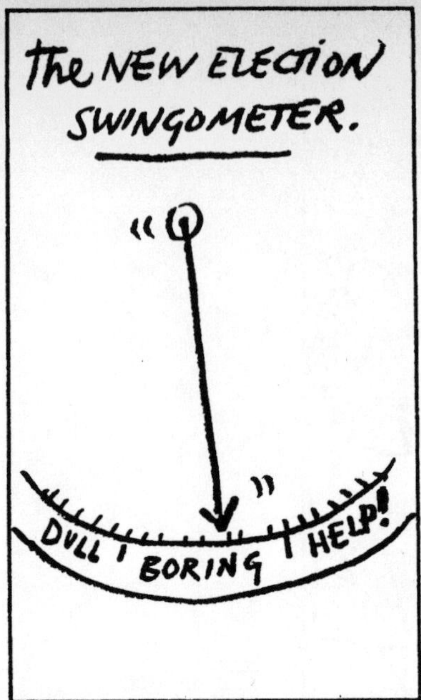


2 April 1992

8 May 1992

12 May 1992

29 May 1992

3 September 1992

10 September 1992

11 November 1992

25 November 1992

9 December 1992

29 January 1993

2 February 1993

16 February 1993

26 February 1993

7 April 1993

22 April 1993

13 May 1993

If it wasn't
for us
CRIMINALS-
you'd be out
of a JOB...


1 July 1993

16 July 1993

Run for your lives- it's one of ours...
UN


31 August 1993

It takes two to make a single MUM...


10 November 1993

24 November 1993

12 January 1994

21 January 1994

3 February 1994

I hear this place
is sicker than
I am...
GUYS


11 February 1994: Labour propose reforms to an NHS suffering from Tory government cuts. Mel's last cartoon

# Affairs of the heart

This series of articles first appeared in *The Times* in 1984, after Mel's first heart 'episode' (as doctors seemed to like to call it), and were later made into a booklet for the Coronary Prevention Group. They seem especially poignant now, in the light of his death ten years later.

A very unfunny thing happened to me on the way to *The Times* a few weeks ago. My doctor told me that I'd had a heart attack. Trust me not to notice. The trouble with being a hypochondriac is that you're so busy worrying about your health, you don't notice the fact that you've had a heart attack.

I had been feeling out of breath when indulging in heavy exercise – like going to the bathroom. And so I'd gone to my doctor for reassurance. 'Just tell me I'm OK please,' I said. Instead of bland reassurance I got an ECG and this deafening news about a heart attack. 'A minor episode' the GP called it. Well, it may have been minor to medical science – but it felt extremely major to me, I can tell you.

'I want you to go to hospital for a check-up,' he said.

'Tomorrow,' I said. 'I must go to work now. They're holding the front page and it's a very heavy thing to hold for longer than ten minutes.'

'Go now,' he said, 'and pack a bag as I expect they'll invite you to stay.' That's the trouble with having so much charm: people keep asking one to stay.

I went home and packed a bag. I wondered if I should ring my lawyer and make a will. Don't be so silly, I said to myself and concentrated on choosing some books to take with me for company. Nothing seemed suitable. Tolstoy seemed too serious and P. G. Wodehouse too frivolous. I settled for Bemelman's *Life Class*. It always makes me laugh – and the title had suitable overtones. I was, as you can see, getting into the right cosmic state of mind.

It was now six o'clock in the evening and the casualty department was not too busy. I tried to phone a friend but the only two phones there were broken. I remembered they were broken the last time I was there about six years ago. If only British Telecom spent less time on Communications and more on telephones . . .

A young doctor of about twenty-three examined me and studied a fresh ECG. 'You might have had a heart attack or you might not. I'll show this to a more senior doctor.' He smiled. I didn't. 'Won't be long.' I lay there, all undressed and shivering with panic on a sort of trolley. I felt like an uncooked fish, waiting for the chef's verdict on how they wanted me served.

A passing nurse remembered my name from the old days when she had been a cashier at my bank, and on the strength of this emotional involvement, offered to get me a cup of tea. She then pulled up the sides of my trolley and I was trapped like a six-year-old in a cot.

I'm afraid I am the second opinion...

While I waited I examined my life and I did not get good marks. I wanted to get my book but the effort of unlocking the bars of my trolley seemed beyond me. I wanted my Mummy and I remembered that she'd gone to the Great Cartoonist in the Sky many years ago. If I get out of this place I said to Him Up There, I will be so *good.* I will eat up all my fibre and take regular exercise, like all the colour magazines say one should. And I will even help old ladies across the road – not just the pretty ones with nice legs.

Him Up There did not reply. As usual he was either not there, or engaged talking to someone else. God is a bit like British Telecom – too busy with astral satellites to bother with mere mortals like you and me.

The Senior Doctor arrived. He was all of twenty-five years old. He also smiled. He thought I might have had a heart attack some weeks ago. 'A minor episode,' he said. Well, if I had learned nothing else this night, it was this new wonderful phrase that covered major fears. I could hardly wait to try it out on someone else.

'Have you any chest pains?' he asked. 'No,' I said firmly. 'You can go home then. Come back to the clinic on Monday.' I dressed quickly before he could change his mind. The time was nearly ten o'clock. I had spent the longest four hours of my life without my clothes on. And it wasn't as much fun as some of the other things you can do without any clothes on.

Several weeks and doctors later I got my instructions. Lose weight. Stop all cholesterol. Take exercise. So it is goodbye to cakes and hello to running shoes. I will report further. I hope to get fit and I expect to hate every minute of it.

## *The day I got my just desserts*

On Sunday I went to a dinner party and instead of looking at the other guests, as I used to do, I looked at the menu. Lean meat (good), boiled potatoes in their skin (very good), ratatouille (excellent) and pudding (help). Pudding was a choice of cheesecake (hundreds of calories) or chocolate mousse (don't even think about it). If I tell you that I regard chocolate mousse with the same kind of lust that I reserve for Meryl Streep and Jane Fonda combined, you will understand the problem I had turning the other cheek to this provocation.

My hostess kindly offered me a half grapefruit as a bribe for not eating the mousse. I devoured the grapefruit – but it was not the same. I watched everyone else eating the mousse and wished I were fourteen again. Of course, when I was fourteen, chocolate was rationed. That's life.

This wrestling with my appetite is proving more difficult than I imagined it would be. I have for most of my adult life enjoyed a pot of tea in the afternoons, preferably accompanied by a slice of fruit cake or some other kind of nourishing devilment. It is a civilized habit, and helps me to prepare myself for the rigours of *The Times* that lie ahead. My new regime dictates that I can have the tea but with no sugar and no cake.

If only the guilt could kill off the cholesterol..


So I sit in my favourite tea shop and try not to look at the pastries on the table in front of me. Opposite me sit a young couple gazing fondly into each other's cakes. I cannot stand this mixture of sex and overt cholesterol. I begin to think everyone else is having a good time except me. To stop this wave of self-pity, I help myself to a 'Veneziana', almost without thinking. A Veneziana is a kind of poem in calories, with a generous sprinkling of white sugar all over the top. It tastes of young lemons and makes you feel the world has some hope left in it.

But the guilt: I could not decide whether to eat the cake slowly to make the wickedness last or quickly in case anyone saw me eating it. I finally decided on a British compromise and ate it medium fast, with lots of nonchalance – the way men in raincoats look at rude magazines in Soho bookshops.

I know now why people diet – it gives them something to talk about. You suddenly belong to a club with hundreds of members. I can discourse at length about what foods I no longer eat and why. I can bore people for twenty minutes about the wickedness of eating eggs or white bread. And in return people can bore me back. I get advice about macrobiotic foods and Indian food and Chinese food and yin and yang. I sometimes long for the bad old days when I could simply eat a large cheese sandwich without feeling I might drop dead the next minute.

And the time it all takes. I now have to read the labels on packages to see what sugar and salt is cunningly concealed in its contents. Oh, those long lost days of innocence when I just grabbed cakes from the supermarket shelves – not to mention eggs and cream and butter and . . . I cannot even write these words now without feeling wicked and guilty. It's like sex used to be when you were twelve. It sounded very exciting, but you knew you were never going to get any. That's how chocolate cake seems to me now. Except that I do have my memories . . .

What about exercise, you ask. Well, I try to walk every day. Pretend I don't have a car. I try to do page one of the Helpful Home Workout Exercises. It's not exactly Jane Fonda aerobic territory yet, but it is a beginning. A helpful friend suggested I walk upstairs to my seventh floor flat instead of using the lift. I tried it the other night and arrived so exhausted I had to cancel my plans for the rest of the evening. 'And what did you do last night, Mel?' 'Well, I walked up seven floors and fell fast asleep afterward.' Wow – some guys have all the fun.

The good news is that I have lost three pounds in four weeks and everyone at *The Times* says I look amazingly healthy. Well, not everyone. The Night Editor doesn't say so, but that's because he still eats crisps and Kit-Kat sandwiches. Lucky man.

## *Tea and sympathy, but no sugar*

I have had lots (well, six or seven) letters from kind readers, offering me sympathy and advice after seeing my heartfelt pieces in *The Times*. I really am both touched and grateful. I never realized quite so many people actually read the paper.

One man sent me a long eulogy about the benefits of Aikido, which is not, as a friend suggested, Japanese sex but a method for throwing people across the room. It makes both the thrower and the throwee extremely fit.

I have, however, reluctantly decided against this pastime. It is tempting but I know my own limitations. One of them is that I hate defying gravity. I don't think God intended us to do that.

I learnt this at school when I was forced to climb ropes. I have no head for heights and always fell straight down to the hard gym floor. Even simple games like leapfrog were beyond me. The only physical exercise I enjoyed was jumping to conclusions – for which I had (and still have) a natural aptitude.

When other boys had to choose teams for anything I was always left to last. It tended to undermine my sense of personal worth. During my National Service in the army I was sent on a special course to the PT School at Shornecliffe, Kent, to learn how to use my limbs properly.

We had to climb up a thirty-foot scaffolding and get down again. I managed to get up, then froze in terror when I looked down and saw the ground. I also saw the military hospital on one side and the military cemetery on the other. The sergeant instructor had to climb up and half-carry me down. This was called 'confidence training'. I never found out why.

Another reader sent me a booklet on 'Deep Relaxation and the Ageing Process'. This was interesting but I felt I most needed a short breath of fresh air. I asked the deputy editor if *The Times* could send me to the Caribbean for two weeks. 'I don't hear so well this morning,' he said.

So I went to Ireland instead. I try to be flexible. I went to a country house hotel run by some friends who understand the art of deep relaxation as no one else I know.

The hotel is a beautiful place: full of peace and quiet and cholesterol. It's like a Temple of Cream. The owner-cook worships at the altar of cream and butter. Butter goes into everything from the soup to the starch they put on the sheets.

One look at the sweet trolley and my blood cells went on strike. 'If that solid cream comes down here,' they said, 'we're all going to clot and then you'll be sorry . . .' So I had fresh raspberries and a peach instead.

Fortunately my daughter, Claire, is a devout cream taster and she described the chocolate ice cream to me. I swear I put on weight just listening to her.

We tried to play tennis every morning to assuage our guilt about the food we were eating – even the fresh air tasted of cream.

It must have been the Irish wind, which is very strong, because I could not seem to get my serves into the correct court. I got the serve into the net very nicely and once into the swimming pool with deadly accuracy but the correct court eluded me. I think John McEnroe can still sleep easy at night.

We also walked. The trouble with walking is that it gives one a terrible appetite. I confess a small piece of ginger cake once passed my lips. But I was desperate and our hosts would have been deeply offended by my refusal.

In spite of this depraved digression from my pure life, I have still lost weight and am now a mere 11 st. 1 lb. For the first time in my adult life I have had to go to a tailor's shop to take in a pair of trousers. From 34 in. to 32 in.

Next week I go back to the clinic to get my cholesterol level checked. I tell you, it is one exciting event after another.

## *My great escape to the tea shop*

People say to me: 'Why don't you go to a Health Farm? If you want to be healthy, that's the place for you.' I once went to a Health Farm. Not for my own sake, you understand, because in those far-off, innocent days I knew I was unhealthy and did not worry about it. It was to keep my then wife company. The irony was that she was extremely healthy. She was strong, vigorous and could carry both our suitcases without getting out of breath. And sometimes had to after I had my hernia. (But that is another story.)

The Health Farm she chose was one of the early pioneer ones, based on the principles of Dr Bircher-Benner. I think he believed everyone should eat ropes and string all day long. And without any sugar – not even the brown sand-like stuff.

The regime there was very strict and one felt like a boarder in a Dickensian school. Even though I was not on the warm water and slice of lemon diet because I had registered myself as a guest and not a

victim, I was still obliged to observe the house rules. No salt was allowed and I remember eating a boiled egg one fine morning (ah, boiled eggs . . . what bliss they were before some idiot discovered there was cholesterol in them, but I digress) and having to beg the waitress for some salt. 'Well, I'll get some,' she whispered, 'but please don't tell anyone.' I never thought it was possible to make *salt* sound sinful.

I remember all the conversations were about food. Large ladies sat sadly nibbling their damp prunes and talked endlessly of fried eggs and crispy bacon. One said: 'I don't know why I'm fat, I never eat anything.' She then proceeded to list what she did eat and it was enough to feed a troop of Cossacks.

Little did I know then that one day I too would have to give up eggs and bacon and salt and find them wicked. I sometimes think that if we knew what treats life held in store for us, we would refuse to grow up.

I also remember wonderful treatments where you put your bottom in cold water and your feet in hot water. And then for a change you had to put your feet in cold water and your bottom in hot water. It must have done something for the staff because it did nothing for me.

The days seemed to stretch out for ever. I got up and avoided thinking about salt and had a walk and read ten books and it was still only 11.30 a.m.

It was like being dead – except that you felt hungry. My then wife had terrible headaches but was convinced that these treatments were doing her good. I considered myself something of an amateur masochist in those days, but this was all too professional for me. It was organized pain and suffering.

I remember escaping one afternoon into the nearest hamlet and gorging myself on tea and scones and butter and jam and cakes. I got so high on all this carbohydrate I thought I'd float away on a cloud of happiness. I have always had simple tastes in depravity.

Why suffer here at vast expense when I can do it at HOME for nothing?


I saw one of the inmates in the same café and he tried to hide behind the menu – but of course, he was too large for that.

I thought of blackmailing him by taking photos of his full frontal assault on the chocolate éclairs but my better nature prevailed.
Anyway I had forgotten to bring my camera with me.

I still think it's Health Farms that give good health a bad name.

## *An amble each day keeps the doctor away*

Middle age has many excitements to offer the unsuspecting male. Flab, greying hair, reading spectacles, shortness of breath and now (sound of trumpets) The Cholesterol Blood Test. No home is complete without one. After the minor episode with my heart all those months ago I have been trying to lower the cholesterol level in my blood. I have given up butter and ice cream and fatty this and fatty that. I have embraced the chicken and the turkey and the fish with the dedicated fervour of a fanatic discovering a new God. And so last week I went in search of a blood test to check the results of all this dietary virtue.

The blood test is a simple affair – it requires a small sample of blood and the ability to remember not to eat or drink anything from midnight the night before.

I got up very early (early for me – around 7.30) and drove to the hospital. I must say that North London, where the hospital lies, is not the cheeriest part of London, especially if you have not eaten any breakfast.

The hospital itself is vaguely modern: straight lines everywhere and an abundance of sage green tiles. I cannot pretend one's heart lifts at the sight of it. (Why are so many hospitals quite so depressing to look at? Surely you need cheering up and not down in hospital.)

I noticed that I was much happier this time than on my previous visits. I had stopped writing my obituary in my head. I felt a great deal lighter in spirit – and in flesh, too.

While I was waiting I overheard two other out-patients talking. Or rather, one was talking and the other was listening. The woman was saying proudly: 'You've not had open heart surgery. I'm sorry to disappoint you. I *have*. What you had was only a vein taken from your leg and put in here,' and she tapped him fiercely in his chest. He blushed with shame. These clinical details were a bit much for me on an empty stomach at 9.30 in the morning, so I went in search of a cup of tea. (I first checked that I could have tea so long as it contained no pleasure, no milk and no sugar.)

I found a small tea bar womanned by two sweet ladies who looked as if they belonged to the WVS. Only white sugar was available, I noticed. (Strange that hospitals don't always practise all that stuff they preach about healthy foods.) There were also some very charming scones, but I resisted their silent overtures.

My blood was taken for the test and I saw my specialist. Notice that all patients refer to 'my specialist'. My mother used to refer to her specialist and then add quickly: 'He's a big man in Harley Street.' I never understood about the magic properties of being big in Harley Street. I expect it referred to the big fees.

My specialist seemed pleased with my weight loss and we had a diverting conversation about fats and cholesterol. I felt like a boy who has been summoned to see the headmaster and hopes he will escape before he is told to do extra prep for the rest of his life. But of course there was talk of extra prep. He told me that I must take more exercise. 'I ask everyone to walk for at least an hour every day knowing that they won't do it. But do aim for an hour.'

I remember how grateful I was to have avoided serious trouble and promised to be good. He nodded benignly and said I need not return for another check-up for nine months. 'We will keep an eye on you. And, of course, if you have any pain or problems call me immediately.'

Or sooner, I said to myself.

## *Taking it all to heart*

Today I looked at myself in the bathroom mirror and wondered who that slim man was standing there. I will not say he looked like Robert Redford but at least he no longer looked like Robert Morley's understudy.

Some sunny days when I am walking along, feeling lighter (after all, I am no longer carrying that large parcel of fat around), I must confess I do feel better. I never thought I'd ever relish feeling healthier.

All my life I have despised people who wanted to be fit. At school the most boring boys were the FIT ones. All my best friends were the unfit ones – the ones you knew were secretly sapping their strength. (At least I hoped they were since I didn't want to be the only one doing it.)

I confess I do feel slightly superior and virtuous as I wave the sugar away and say '*No*' to the pudding trolley, although I still look at it wistfully. The occasional treats now seem so wicked and twice as enjoyable as they used to be. The flavour of sin has been added to ice cream.

The major difference between my present regime and any past attempts to reduce weight is that I feel my life depends on it, and that, as Doctor Johnson probably said, concentrates the diet wonderfully.

I mean, life is difficult, confusing, frustrating and chaotic, but what would I do without it? Death must be terribly boring – especially on Saturday nights. And apart from my family and friends, I'd miss all the aggravations of trying to please editors.

I would also miss looking at women. Thank God there is no cholesterol in women. At least he got something right. (What he was doing putting cholesterol into ice cream and chocolate, I'll never know. He should have put it into something boring like coal dust.)

I recently re-read some wise words by Professor Nixon, who knows a thing or two about hearts, in a book called *The BMA Book of Executive Health*. Ironically enough, I read the book some five years ago because I had to illustrate it. Needless to say, I ignored the message of the words. I did not think they applied to me.

All that stuff about fatigue, tension, diet, relaxation and sleep applied to executives, not to cartoonists. I was far too lazy, I thought, to suffer from stress and overwork. Looking back I now recognize what Professor Nixon calls the danger signs: a cycle of fatigue and a consequent need to do more to prove to yourself that you can cope with your problems.

It is a bit like driving through a red light – if you don't hit anything you are tempted to go on doing it. Other people have accidents, not you. Other people have heart attacks, not me.

So I have discovered that I am incredibly mortal. I am not protected by some special magic. My arteries are not designed to be abused. For all I know, they are not designed at all – they just lie there, all tangled up.

What I am having (very reluctantly) to come to terms with is that I am a body as well as a mind. I have to listen to, and respect my body, or else it will sabotage me. It is no use having some intelligence (what intelligence, you ask?) if I am not going to use it to try to live sensibly. Half a roll is better than none at all, I suppose. Even if the half a roll is spread with polyunsaturated margarine instead of butter.

# Calman, God and the Devil

The cartoons about God in this section have been selected from *My God* (1970), a book that – far from being thought blasphemous – seems to be particularly popular with the clergy.

The Adam and Eve strip, which appeared in *Town & Country* magazine, was called variously 'The First Couple' and 'Calman in Eden'.

*My God*

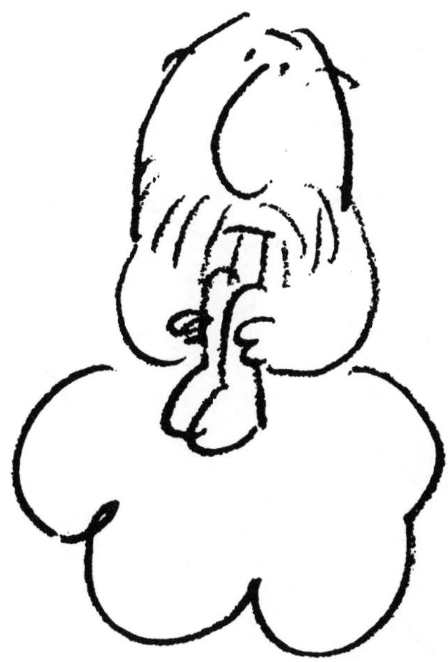
one week's work
and an eternity
of worry...

I think I've lost my copy of The Divine Plan

I may not be perfect but I'm better than nothing...

Please God!
Help!

Why can't I have someone to pray to?

Help me!
Help! Please

I don't seem to be
as omnipotent as
I used to be ...

I should have known –
create in haste,
repent at leisure . .

Love one another
or I'll come down there
and thump you . . .

Of course, once you've created The Universe, everything else you do seems an anti-climax...

I'd like to retire -
but what else
could I do?

I wonder what would have happened if I'd had a DAUGHTER instead?

Eternity is a long time
to have to stay in
one job..

# The first couple

## As it was in the beginning . . .

Who are you?
I'm WOMAN! EVE... from the Deity that gave you Paradise
I'm going to lighten your days, make joyous your nights, enrich your life...
But first I must wash my hair

I'm depressed!
Day after day - just you and me, me and you..
I'm sick of Paradise - I want to see the World..
It's places like this that drive people to Sin..

Hello sexy! How about a nice apple?
You're Evil - trying to tempt an innocent girl
You're bound to get some consumer resistance with a new product..

No! God doesn't want me to eat it
God doesn't EXIST. He's only a projection of your Unconscious..
Not only are you very wicked and Evil, you're even worse..
You're an Intellectual!

The Serpent has invited us over to his place for supper
He wants us to try a new dish - it's called 'Adam's Apple'
Never mind the flattery - We're not going!
O.K. O.K. Anyway - I haven't got a thing to wear

Pst! How about a spot of adultery?
Impossible! I'm faithful to Eve -
We have this really beautiful relationship..
based on the monogamous concept..
SISH!
And where on earth would I find another woman?

Calman goes to the Devil

Filth!
THE BIBLE

This Permissive Society is taking all the pleasure out of my work

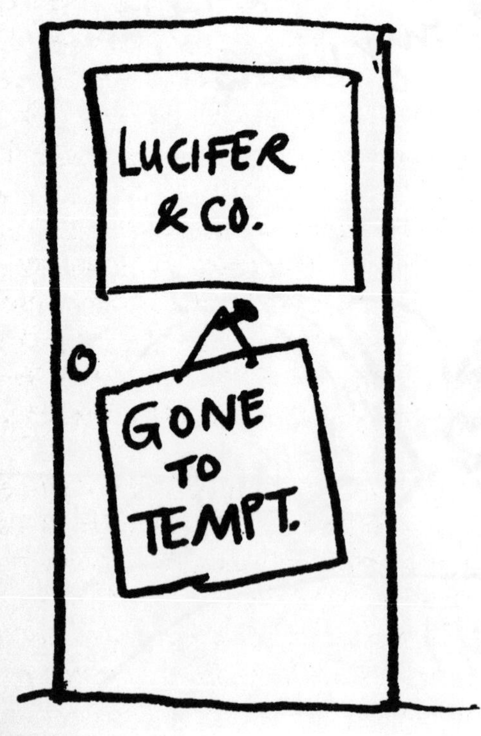
LUCIFER
& CO.
GONE
TO
TEMPT.

# Scenes from *The Big Novel*

Given that much of a cartoonist's skill lies in saying a lot in as few words as possible, it is hardly surprising that cartoonists rarely try their hand at novel-writing. Mel disliked even reading long books never mind trying to write one. (Nor did he like sitting through long films: he used to emerge from the cinema muttering 'Good, but too long' and snip his fingers together like scissors, eager to excise every extraneous second.) He found, however, his own format – a narrative cartoon novel, not a comic strip. I have selected two extracts: one from the beginning of the book, the other (starting here on p. 232) from the end.

The
sun
rose...

but he didn't ...

INSTEAD –

He turned over

and thought about THE BIG NOVEL...

it will be wonderful..
RICH.. MOVING..
poetic..
insightful..
IRONIC..
compassionate..
tender.. even
funny.. sexy..
the best..
BOOKER PRIZE..
FAME! GLORY!
WOMEN! Money!
and WOMEN!

But first a little rest –

TOMORROW I will start..
TOMORROW..
TOMORROW..

Z

Z

Z

Z Z

TOMORROW comes...

as TOMORROWS tend to do...

There are so many things
I must do TODAY.. do some
SHOPPING (NO MILK).. go to
The LAUNDERETTE (no clean shirts)
take the CAR in (no exhaust)
Phone the dentist (no gums
soon..)

I bet JANE AUSTEN never had to go the LAUNDERETTE – or TOLSTOY to the GARAGE to have his car fixed..

I suppose I could
go through my old DIARIES
and notebooks and search
for a PLOT..

There was Helen.. she was
a NOVEL in herself..

Helen..
let me see..
I could write
about
:
Is this
FLASHBACK
time?

What's wrong with FLASHBACKS?
I've had a VERY interesting
life..

its the OLD
NOSTALGIA
but, is it?
The FIFTIES.
PARIS, youth,
oh dear.. dear..

you're so hard to PLEASE..
at least it's a start.
it's a BEGINNING..

CHAPTER ONE

TAP!
TAP!

Call me
when you
need a
CRIT.

All that summer he yearned for someone to love..

It was one of those parties where people kept saying 'hello' and then moving on before he could say 'hello' back. This was the permissive sixties, he thought, and still no-one had given him permission to be permissive. The only joy that night had been a long-jawed girl who worked as a researcher for the BBC. She had pressed against him when he was trying to spoon some of the fruit punch into his glass without covering himself with pieces of orange peel. Philip knew her from some other party but before he could recollect her name she had moved on and was now thrusting her long jaw up against an account executive from Collett, Dickenson and Pearce. The account executive was married to an Earth Mother who lectured in anthropology and taught the Alexander Technique in her spare time. He hated parties, but still went to them in his mad desire to meet female flesh.

It was a mistake. He would have just one more glass of the fruit poison and go home. A Beatles record was playing somewhere down in the basement and Philip considered moving towards the thudding sound. The host worked for The Sunday Times and had written a long profile on the Beatles.

In the far corner of the open-plan kitchen/ diner Philip could see a promising novelist (his novel about a Northern footballer who had his balls transplanted from a young bullock had attracted considerable critical acclaim) manoeuvering his hands down the front of an actress who had once done the voice-over for a Heinz commercial.

Philip felt slightly sick. He tried to rmemeber where the loo was. The thought of the avocado coloured basin made him feel even sicker..

STOP! No-one will pay money to read this escapist RUBBISH! The world is in a frightful state – INFLATION! Unemployment! NUCLEAR MADNESS! Herpes! – and you write of sixties parties! Have you no sense of shame? Do try to be LESS TRIVIAL, for GOD'S SAKE!

A CRITIC ↑

TAP! TAP!

SORRY!
SORRY!
I will try to be less
trivial - but LIFE is
trivial - it's BILLS and
TOOTHACHE and
INSOMNIA.. it's NOT
EPIC VERSE, you know -
it's NOT TROILUS and
CRESSIDA - it's
PARKING TICKETS..

Here I am
down in this PIT
of DEPRESSION and
you tell me to observe
the STARS.. I don't
WANT advice -
I WANT the name
of a good AGENT!
....

SNORT!
WHO NEEDS it?
If it wasn't for SUPEREGOS like that - I would not be where I am TODAY..

And with an
ALMIGHTY BOUND
he sprang FREE!

There's always tomorrow..

The day I do my
best writing..

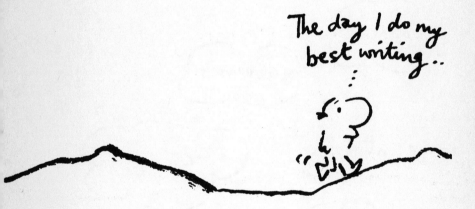

*The Big Novel* continued

The NEXT DAY...

Chapter One

All that summer he yearned for sex...

It was one of those parties where people kept saying 'hello' and you can do it!

Do you really THINK SO?

you can do it!
THINK of the FOYLES LITERARY LUNCH!
The BOOKER PRIZE!!
JUST GO FORWARD!
ALL TOGETHER NOW!

GO FORWARD...

one page ... at a time ...

RUMBLE!

ANGST..
etc

BANG!
LIFE..
etc
BANG!
LOVE..
ETC

LAWYERS

ACCOUNTANTS

POLITICIANS

Why do we do this?

It's a LIVING..